My First
Story Bible

Tim Dowley

Illustrated by Roger Langton

CANDLE
BOOKS

Old Testament

New Testament

The Beginning
In the beginning there was nothing at all.

Then God said, "Let there be light!"
At once there was light.

1

Then God put water into the sea and clouds into the sky.

God made the land: green hills and river valleys.

God put the sun in the sky to make day,
and the moon and stars to give light by night.

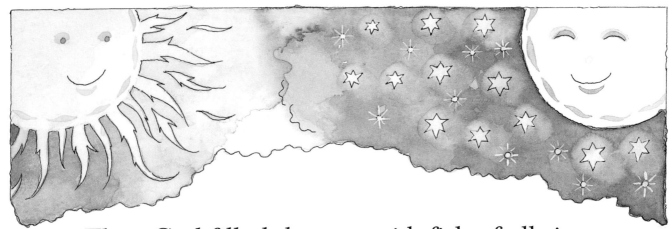

Then God filled the seas with fish of all sizes
and the sky with birds of all kinds.

Next God made all sorts of different animals.
And finally he made the first man, called Adam.

Everything God made was just right.

Adam and Eve

God gave Adam a beautiful garden called Eden.

But Adam was lonely living alone in the garden.
So God made a woman, called Eve.

"Enjoy the garden," God told Adam.
"But *never ever* eat fruit from that special tree."

Then one day a snake slithered sneakily up to Eve.

"Take a bite of that fruit," the serpent whispered.
"But God told us never to do that," answered Eve.

But even so, Eve took the fruit and bit into it.
And Adam had some too.

So God sent Adam and Eve out of the beautiful garden.
They were both very sad.

Noah

Soon there were lots and lots of people living on the earth. But they were unkind and cruel.

"I shall send a flood to wash my world clean," God said.

But there lived one good man. His name was Noah.
God said, "Noah, you must build a huge boat."

When Noah at last finished hammering and sawing,
God said, "Now you must find two of every animal."

So Noah took all these animals and his family into the ark.

Then the rain started. And didn't stop!
Soon Noah's ark was floating on the water.

But all the people and animals inside the ark were safe.

When the flood was over, God put a beautiful rainbow into the sky, saying, "Never again will I flood all the earth."

A Great Tower

One day some people started to build a huge, tall tower. "Let's see if we can reach heaven," they said.

But God was angry when he saw what they were doing.

So God made all of them speak different languages.
No one could understand anyone else – and no one knew
what to do next. So the tower never got finished.

It was called the "Tower of Babel".

Abraham

In a far-off land lived a man named Abraham.
One day God said, "I'm going to give you a special land."

So Abraham packed his bags, loaded his animals and set
out with his family to discover this special land.

After journeying for many, many months, Abraham came at last to the land God had promised him.

And there he settled down with his wife, Sarah.

"Look up!" God said to Abraham one night. "Can you count the stars? One day there will be more people in your family than there are stars in the sky!"

The Twin Boys

Now Abraham's son, Isaac, had twin sons
named Esau and Jacob.

Esau was a bold huntsman; but Jacob,
the younger twin, was born crafty.

One day Jacob went to his old, blind father pretending to be Esau. So Isaac gave his special blessing to Jacob instead of Esau.

Esau was so angry that Jacob had to run away from home.

One night, as he slept outdoors on a rock, Jacob dreamt
he saw angels climbing a ladder to heaven.
God promised Jacob, "I will always look after your family."

Joseph the Dreamer

Many years later, Jacob made up with Esau and came back to the Promised Land. Jacob now had twelve sons.

But Jacob loved one son the most. He was called Joseph. Jacob gave him a bright coat. How smart!

. . . And how jealous Joseph's brothers became!

One day they kidnapped Joseph and sold him to traders.
They told Jacob that Joseph was dead. How he wept!

The traders took Joseph to Egypt. He had lots of adventures. First he worked as a servant – then he got thrown into jail.

Finally Joseph became the king of Egypt's chief helper!

One year no rain fell. No one had enough to eat. But in Egypt, Joseph had cleverly stored up grain in great barns.

When old Jacob heard, he took his family to Egypt to find food. How glad he was to find his son Joseph again too!

Moses Escapes from Egypt

Joseph's family stayed in Egypt. They were called "Hebrews". Many years later a new king ruled.

He made the Hebrews work very hard for him.

The cruel king thought there were too many Hebrews. "Kill all the Hebrew baby boys," he shouted.

But one Hebrew mother hid her little baby, Moses,
in a basket.

The princess of Egypt discovered the basket floating in the
river. She saved Moses and brought him up in the palace.

When Moses grew up, he ran away to the desert.
But God spoke to him from a burning bush,
"Go and tell Pharaoh, king of Egypt: 'Let my people go!'"

Moses went to Pharaoh many times.
"Let my people go!" he demanded.

At last Pharaoh gave in.
"Go – and take your people with you!" he cried.

At last Moses' people could set out for
the land God had promised them.

They had to cross the great Red Sea.
God made a dry path through it.

The Hebrews stayed in the desert many years.
They grumbled and moaned and moped.

They even bowed down to a golden calf instead of God.

One day Moses climbed a very high mountain.
He came down again carrying two huge stones.

On the stones God's special rules were written.
We call them the "Ten Commandments".

Then God told Moses, "Build a special big tent where the people can pray to God."

When the Hebrews journeyed on,
they packed up the great tent and carried it with them.

Finally the people got close to the Promised Land.
Moses sent spies ahead to find out more about it.

Two spies came back saying,
"There is a lot of fruit and grain in the Promised Land."

After Moses died, the Hebrews at last came to the Promised Land. God gave them special instructions about how to attack the great city of Jericho.

They walked around and around it. Then the trumpeters blew and the people shouted – and the walls fell down!

Gideon

After they captured the Promised Land –
"Israel" – the Hebrews were called "Israelites".

God gave them some special leaders. One was named Gideon.

God helped Gideon beat the Israelites' enemies.
The soldiers attacked at night, and scared them with
flames and lots of noise!

The enemies ran off terrified.

But still people weren't happy. "Give us a king!" they demanded. "Everyone else has a king."

King Saul

God sent a man called Samuel to find a man fit to be king. He found a very tall man called Saul.

Samuel poured oil on Saul's head,
to show God had chosen him to be king.

At first King Saul ruled well and beat many enemies.

But later Saul disobeyed God,
so Samuel had to find another king.

King David

Now Samuel found a shepherd boy named David.

Although he was still young,
God chose him to become king.

David was very brave. He fought the giant Goliath.
He flung a stone from his sling and killed him.

King David became a great ruler.
He loved to play his harp and sing about God's love.

King Solomon

When David died, his son Solomon became king.
He prayed, "God help me to be fair to my people."

Solomon was very wise.

When people had problems,
they came to ask Solomon what to do.

The Queen of Sheba, who lived far away, heard of
King Solomon. She journeyed for weeks to visit him.

King Solomon built a beautiful new temple.
It was made from the best gold, wood and stone.

The People Disobey God

But after Solomon, many bad kings ruled Israel.
The people broke many of God's laws.

God sent special messengers, called prophets,
to tell them to return to God's way.

One prophet, Elijah, went to see wicked King Ahab.

"Worship the living God," said Elijah. When Elijah prayed, God sent fire on the altar he had built.

God sent many other prophets: Jeremiah, Isaiah and a shepherd prophet called Amos.

They warned, "If you don't mend your ways, God will send enemies to beat you. You will be scattered over the earth!"

But the people didn't listen. Cruel kings came from Assyria and Babylon and carried them off.

They destroyed the beautiful city of Jerusalem.

Daniel and the Lions

Daniel was wise and helped the king of Babylon.
One day the king made a new law.
"Everyone must pray to me alone."

But Daniel still prayed to God.

Some sneaky men told the king,
so he threw Daniel into a den of lions!

"God, please save me!" prayed Daniel.

And God shut the lions' mouths. They didn't touch Daniel.

Jonah and the Huge Fish

One day, God told the prophet Jonah, "Go to Nineveh.
Tell the people to stop doing bad things."

But Jonah was scared – so he took a boat going the other way!

A storm blew up, and the sailors threw him into the sea.

God sent an enormous fish to swallow Jonah.

After three days, the fish spat him out on the seashore.

Jonah learnt his lesson.
Now he went to Nineveh, as God told him.

A Special Promise

But prophets also said,
"God still loves you, in spite of your bad ways.
He will send a special person who will save you."

Many years later that special person came,
just as God promised. His name was Jesus.

An Angel Visits Mary

Long ago, in the time of King Herod of Judea,
there lived a girl called Mary.

One day God sent the
angel Gabriel to Mary.
"Don't be afraid!" he said.
"God is pleased with you.
He is going to give you a
very special baby. You
must call him Jesus!"

Then the Angel
disappeared.
But Mary was very happy.
She sang a song to thank God.

64

Mary married Joseph, the village carpenter.

They began to get ready for the baby.

It was almost time for Mary's baby to be born.

Then the governor of the country decided
to count all the people.

Mary and Joseph Travel to Bethlehem

So Mary and Joseph went
on a long journey, to a town called
Bethlehem, to be counted.

When at last they arrived in Bethlehem,
Mary was very tired.
Joseph knocked at the
door of an inn.

"No room!" said the man.
So they had to sleep in a stable.

Jesus is Born

That night, with the donkey and cows standing close,
Mary's baby boy, Jesus, was born.

In fields nearby,
shepherds were looking after their sheep.

Suddenly an angel appeared. The shepherds were scared.
"Don't be afraid!" said the angel.

"Tonight a special baby has been born in Bethlehem.
He will save his people."
Then crowds of singing angels filled the air.

The angels disappeared as quickly as they
had come. All was dark again.

The shepherds rushed off into Bethlehem.
They had to find the new baby!

The shepherds soon found Mary and Joseph
in the stable – and baby Jesus lying in a manger.

Wise Men Bring Gifts to Jesus

At the time that Jesus was born,
in a far country, wise men
were looking at the night sky.

"Look!" said one, "I've never seen that star before."

"It means a new king has been born,"
said a second.

"We must follow the star and find him,"
said the third wise man.

So the wise men set out on a long, hard journey,
following the star by night.

When they arrived in Judea, they went
straight to King Herod's palace.
But the new king was not there.

At last the star stopped over Bethlehem.

As soon as they saw little Jesus,
the wise men knelt down.

They knew he was the new king.
They gave him rich presents: gold, frankincense and myrrh.

Jesus in the Temple

When Jesus was twelve, his parents took him to Jerusalem.

But they lost him in the crowds.

At last they found Jesus again.
He was talking to the Jewish teachers in the Temple.
They were amazed at the wise things he said.

As he grew up, Jesus knew
that God had a special job for him.

John Baptizes Jesus

Crowds of people went to hear a man called John preach in the desert.

He dipped them in the river Jordan to show that they were making a clean start.

One day Jesus came and said to John, "Baptize me, too."
So John dipped Jesus in the river Jordan.

When Jesus came out of the water, a dove appeared.
God said, "You are my son. I am pleased with you."

Jesus Calls his Disciples

Jesus called twelve men to be his special friends.
Some were fishermen on Lake Galilee.

They visited little villages and big cities.

Jesus told people special stories about how God wants
our world to be.

People were amazed when they listened to him.
Many followed him.

The Lost Sheep

Jesus told a story about a shepherd who had 100 sheep.

One day he lost one. He went searching for it all night.

At last the shepherd found the lost sheep. He was so happy!

Jesus said that God is happy when anyone turns to him.

The Good Samaritan

Jesus told the story of a man
who was on a long journey.
Robbers beat him and stole
everything he had.

He cried out for help.

A priest passed by… A temple servant passed by.

Then a man from another country stopped and helped him.

Jesus said that the man who helped was a kind stranger.

Jesus Heals a Sick Man

One day Jesus was teaching lots of people in a house.
Some men came carrying a sick friend.

But they couldn't get into the house. It was too full.

The friends made a hole in the roof and lowered the sick man.

Jesus knew that they believed he could heal the man.
He said, "Get up and walk!"

At once the man stood up, picked up his bed and went home.

He thanked God for making him better.

Jesus Feeds a Crowd

One day, lots of people went into the country to listen to
Jesus. They began to feel hungry. Jesus' friends said, "We can't
feed them all!"

But one boy gave Jesus his lunch – five bread rolls and two fish. Jesus handed them out. There was enough for everyone!

Jesus Helps a Little Girl

A little girl lived beside Lake Galilee.
One day she fell ill. Her father went to fetch Jesus.
When they got back, the girl had died.

But Jesus said, "Get up, my dear!" And the little girl opened her eyes. "Now get her something to eat," said Jesus.

Jesus Calms a Storm

Once Jesus was sailing with his friends. He fell asleep.
Then a great storm arose. His friends were very scared.

They woke Jesus. "Calm down!" he said to the wind
and the waves. And everything was still again.

Jesus of Nazareth was the friend of many.
He told great stories.

He healed sick people and did wonderful miracles.

Jesus Rides into Jerusalem

There was an important festival in Jerusalem.
Jesus went with twelve special friends, his disciples.

Jesus borrowed a donkey and rode into Jerusalem.
The crowds became very excited.
They shouted and waved palm-tree branches.

But some of the priests hated Jesus
and plotted to kill him.

A Special Supper

On the day of the festival,
Jesus ate a special supper
with his disciples in an upstairs room.

Jesus broke bread and gave it to his disciples.
But one disciple, Judas, was plotting against him.

He crept out.

Jesus is Arrested

After supper, Jesus took his disciples to a garden outside the city. "Stay here and pray," he told them.

Jesus prayed too.
Then a crowd of Jesus' enemies appeared, led by Judas.

The soldiers took Jesus away.

They stood Jesus before the Roman ruler, Pilate.

"Jesus is a troublemaker," said the priest. "He should be killed!"

"I can find nothing wrong with him," said Pilate.

But the people shouted, "*Kill him, kill him!*" So Pilate sent Jesus to die.

110

Cruel men pushed a crown made of thorns on Jesus' head.
Then thcy led him out of the city.

When they reached a hill,
soldiers nailed Jesus to a wooden cross.
Jesus said, "Father, forgive them."

At midday the sky went dark. Jesus cried out and died.
Jesus' family and friends watched sadly.

A good man called Joseph took Jesus' body. He put it in a rock tomb and rolled a huge stone across the door.

Good News!

Early on Sunday morning, women went to the tomb.
The stone was rolled away – but they couldn't see Jesus' body.
A shining man said, "Jesus isn't here! He is risen from the dead."

The women rushed back to tell the disciples.
At first they didn't believe the women.

But then Jesus
appeared to them.

And after that
Jesus appeared to many
of his friends.

Once, Jesus cooked breakfast for his disciples
beside a lake.

A few weeks later, Jesus was taken up into heaven again. The disciples watched.

Peter and John Help a Man

One day, Peter and John went to the temple to pray.

A man who couldn't walk sat outside.
"Give me money!" he begged.

"We have no money," said Peter. "But God will heal you."

The man stood up. Now he could walk!

A Man from Africa Hears about Jesus

A man from Africa was driving his chariot home.

He was reading his Bible. But what did it all mean?

Then he met Philip, one of Jesus' followers.
Philip helped him understand what he was reading.

The man said to Philip,
"I would like to be a friend of Jesus too."

Saul Meets Jesus

Saul hated Jesus and his friends. One day, he set out for the city of Damascus to catch Jesus' friends there.

On his way, a bright light shone.
Saul fell to the ground. "I am Jesus!" said a voice.
"By hurting my friends, you're hurting me."

After this, Saul became one of Jesus' friends too. He
changed completely. He even changed his name to Paul!

Paul and Barnabas Go on a Journey

Now Paul wanted to tell others about Jesus.

With a friend called Barnabas, he walked for miles.

At each place they visited,
Paul and Barnabas told people about Jesus.

Paul Goes to Jail

Later, Paul visited many places with another man, Silas. In one town, they were thrown into jail. They had done nothing wrong – they had just talked about Jesus.

Paul and Silas sang songs about Jesus all night!

Suddenly, at midnight, the earth shook.
The walls cracked. Their chains fell off.

But Paul and Silas didn't run away. The jailer was amazed. He asked, "How can I follow Jesus too?"

Paul is Shipwrecked

Paul set sail on a long voyage.

A storm arose.
The waves crashed – and finally, the ship sank.

But God kept Paul and everyone else on board safe.

Later, Paul and Peter and some of Jesus' other friends wrote down everything they knew about Jesus.

We can read their storics in our Bible.

We remember that Jesus was born in Bethlehem.
And that Jesus died.

And that he is alive for ever.

TO Dominic

Love Your
Godfather
Uncle Chris
Auntie Beata, Lauren, Julia
Elizabeth + Victoria